The Incas
AND THEIR
Road System

The Inca People Grade 4 |
Children's Ancient History

First Edition, 2020

Published in the United States by Speedy Publishing LLC, 40 E Main Street, Newark, Delaware 19711 USA.

© 2020 Baby Professor Books, an imprint of Speedy Publishing LLC

Baby Professor Books are available at special discounts when purchased in bulk for industrial and sales-promotional use. For details contact our Special Sales Team at Speedy Publishing LLC, 40 E Main Street, Newark, Delaware 19711 USA. Telephone (888) 248-4521 Fax: (210) 519-4043.

10 9 8 7 6 * 5 4 3 2 1

Print Edition: 9781541953581
Digital Edition: 9781541956582
Hardcover Edition: 9781541979857

See the world in pictures. Build your knowledge in style.
www.speedypublishing.com

Table of Contents

More than 3,500 years ago, the Incan Empire of South America was flourishing in the Andes Mountains. The Incan Empire grew very large, covering an area of more than two thousand miles and extending into present-day Peru, Chile, Argentina, Bolivia, Ecuador, and Colombia. The Incan people were accomplished engineers[1] and built many impressive cities. But what is particularly notable is the system of roads that the Incans built. While we have modern roads that crumble into potholes after a few years, the Incans were able to construct roads that are still in good working condition today. Let's see how.

---

[1]   Engineer – A person experienced or trained in building design and construction.

ANCIENT PAVED INCAN ROAD ON THE EL CHORO TREK
IN THE ANDES MOUNTAINS NEAR LA PAZ, BOLIVIA.

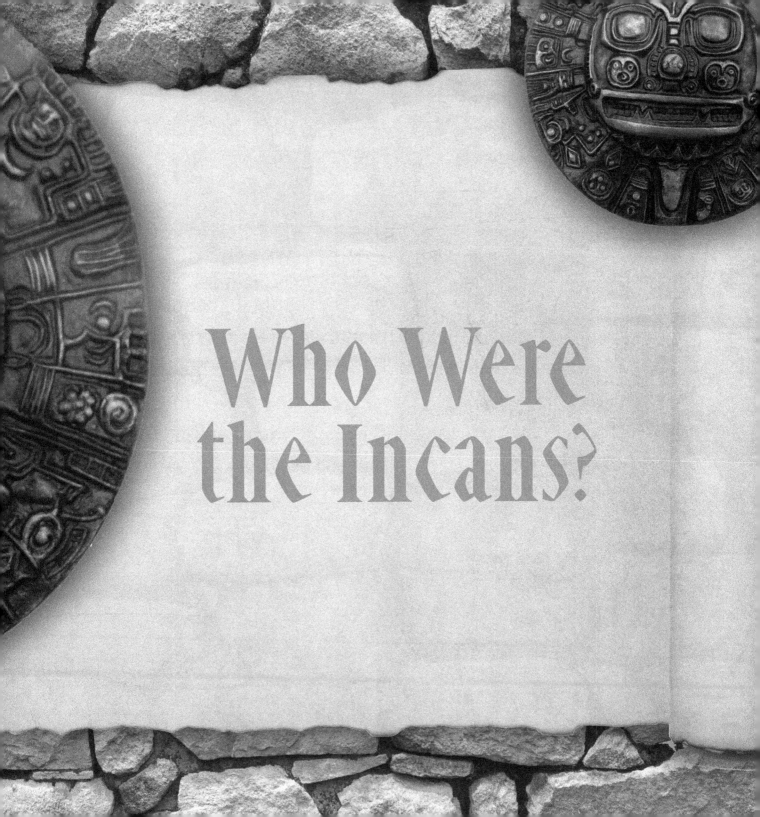

Who Were the Incans?

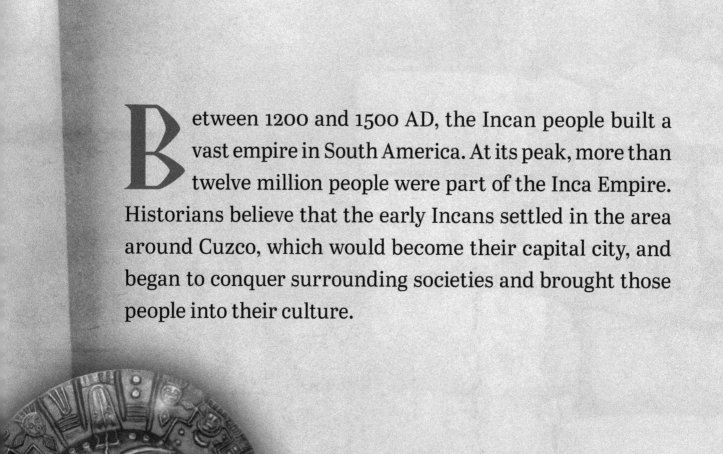

Between 1200 and 1500 AD, the Incan people built a vast empire in South America. At its peak, more than twelve million people were part of the Inca Empire. Historians believe that the early Incans settled in the area around Cuzco, which would become their capital city, and began to conquer surrounding societies and brought those people into their culture.

EARLY INCANS SETTLED IN THE AREA AROUND CUZCO.

MACHU PICCHU, PERU, SOUTH AMERICA

10

The Incas built numerous sprawling cities on the slopes of the Andes Mountains. Archaeologists continue to study the stone ruins of the ancient Incan cities, including the famous Machu Picchu, to learn about this pre-Colombian culture.

The End of
the Incas

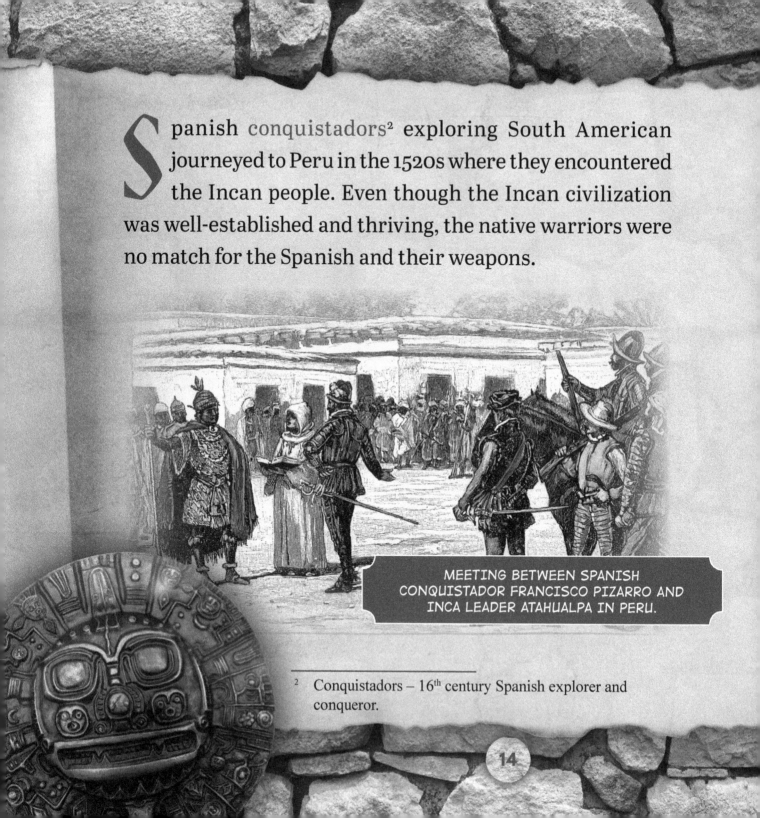

Spanish conquistadors[2] exploring South American journeyed to Peru in the 1520s where they encountered the Incan people. Even though the Incan civilization was well-established and thriving, the native warriors were no match for the Spanish and their weapons.

MEETING BETWEEN SPANISH CONQUISTADOR FRANCISCO PIZARRO AND INCA LEADER ATAHUALPA IN PERU.

[2] Conquistadors – 16th century Spanish explorer and conqueror.

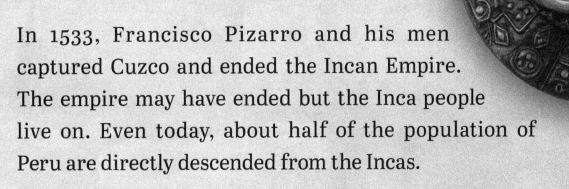

In 1533, Francisco Pizarro and his men captured Cuzco and ended the Incan Empire. The empire may have ended but the Inca people live on. Even today, about half of the population of Peru are directly descended from the Incas.

ATAHUALPA, LORD OF THE INCA EMPIRE, WAS ATTACKED AND CAPTURED BY SPANISH CONQUISTADORS UNDER FRANCISCO PIZARRO.

A Need For Roads

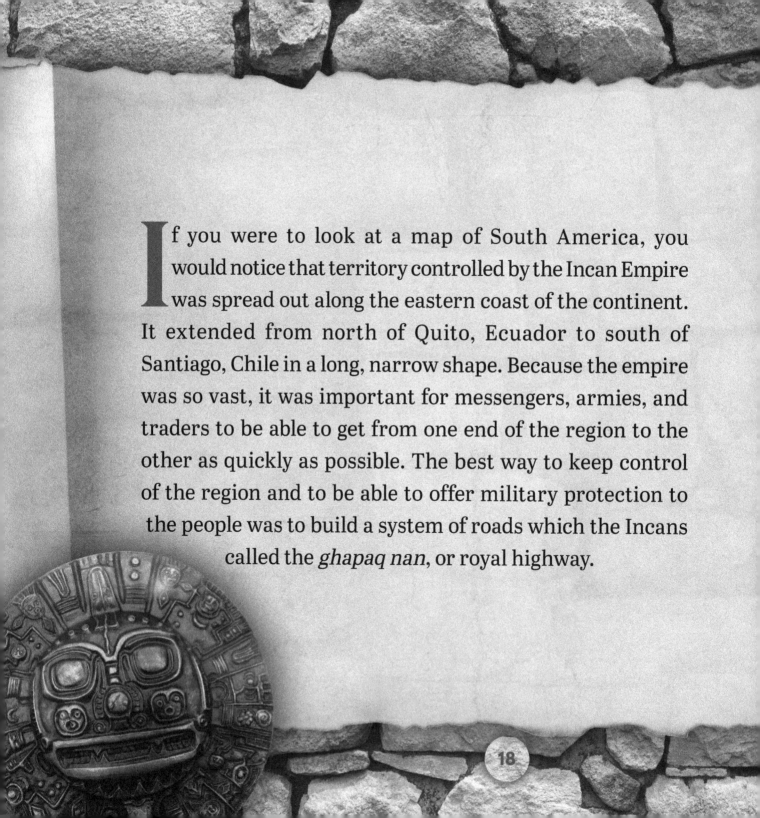

If you were to look at a map of South America, you would notice that territory controlled by the Incan Empire was spread out along the eastern coast of the continent. It extended from north of Quito, Ecuador to south of Santiago, Chile in a long, narrow shape. Because the empire was so vast, it was important for messengers, armies, and traders to be able to get from one end of the region to the other as quickly as possible. The best way to keep control of the region and to be able to offer military protection to the people was to build a system of roads which the Incans called the *ghapaq nan*, or royal highway.

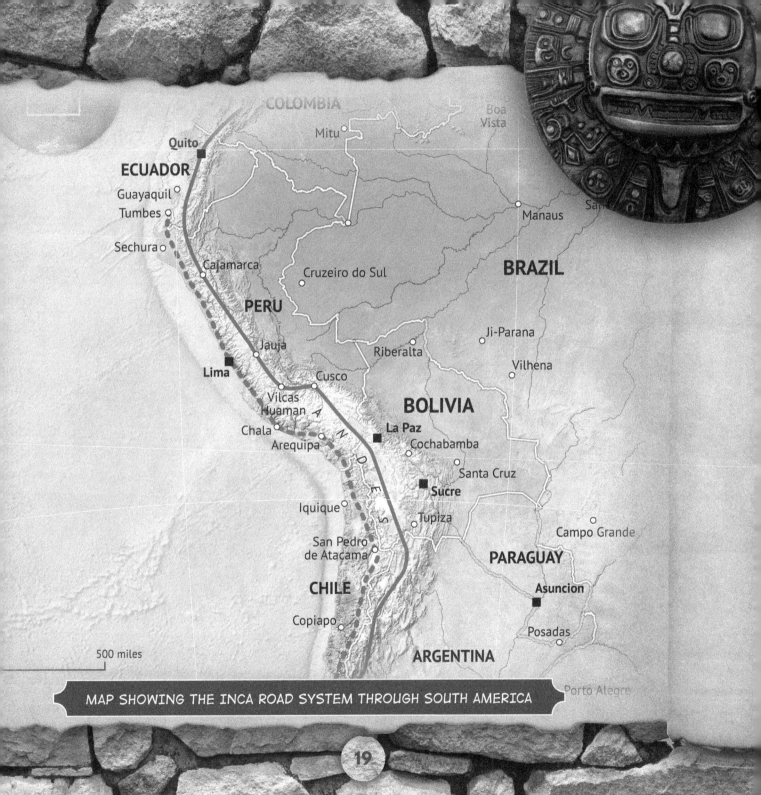

MAP SHOWING THE INCA ROAD SYSTEM THROUGH SOUTH AMERICA

Diverse Terrain

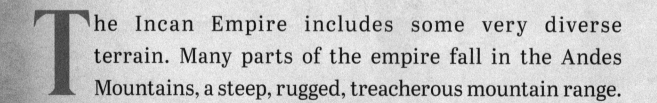

The Incan Empire includes some very diverse terrain. Many parts of the empire fall in the Andes Mountains, a steep, rugged, treacherous mountain range.

TERRACES AND THE ROAD IN THE ANDES

Other parts are in desert regions, including the Atacama Desert. Still other parts are forested or include flat, open plains.

INCA ROAD SYSTEM, ATACAMA DESERT, CHILE

Road buildings materials and techniques would need to be adapted to the different environments and regions if the road system was to be successful. Fortunately, the incredible Incan engineers were able to construct roads that made the best use of the surrounding terrain and natural materials.

SINUOUS INCA ROAD ON THE PERUVIAN SIDE OF LAKE TITICACA

25

A Vast Network of Roads

In all, the Incas constructed more than 25,000 miles of roads. One of the major roads hugged the Pacific coast while a second highway wove through the mountains and highlands. Medium-sized roads connected these two main thoroughfares in a crisscross pattern while additional smaller roads led to villages and administrative centers. The Incas even built roads that extended outside their own territory. This may have been done to make trade easier, but it is also likely that it was a way for the Incas to flex their military might and to facilitate attacks.

THE INCA COASTAL ROAD AT THE PACHACAMAC SANCTUARY, PERU

Not Just Roads

In addition to the roads that were built, the Incas also included bridges over rivers and waterways, causeways[3] over swampy or marshy lands, and stairs cut into mountains and cliffs.

STEPS CUT INTO THE NATIVE MOUNTAINSIDE FOR THE INCA ROAD LEADING TO MACHU PICCHU.

---

[3]   Causeway – A low road over water or wetlands.

Along the roads, which led from one village to another, they added a series of rest stations with shelters, called *chaskiwasi*, where travelers could stop for the night in relative safety. Some of these shelters grew to be quite large and impressive, offering travelers more luxurious accommodations for the night. The chaskiwasi were positioned at roughly twelve-mile increments[4].

AN INCA REST STATION ON THE INCA TRAIL, PERU.

---

[4] Increment – A series at regular intervals.

Varied Building Techniques

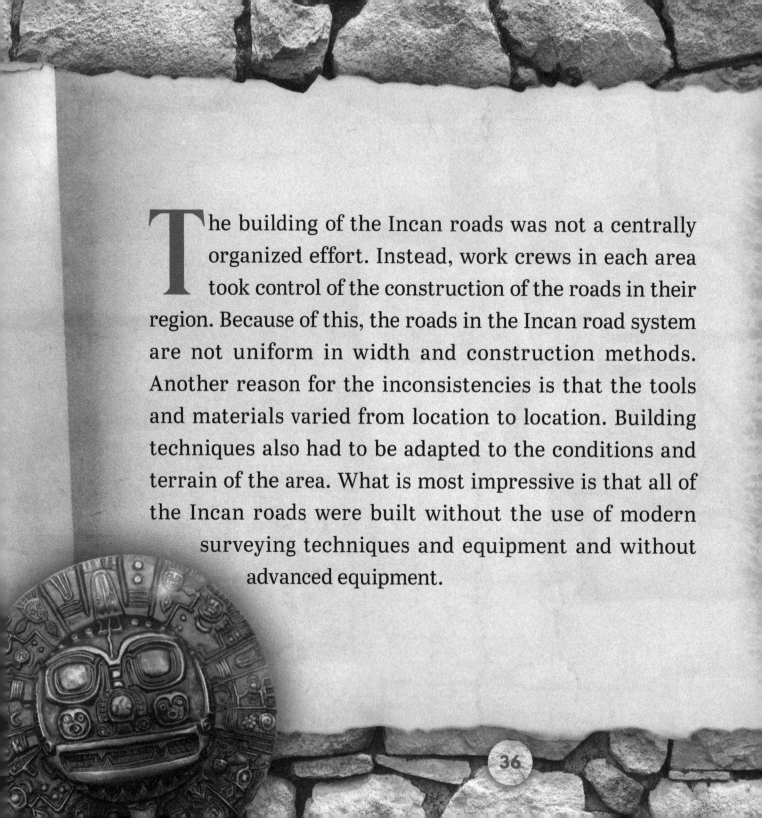

The building of the Incan roads was not a centrally organized effort. Instead, work crews in each area took control of the construction of the roads in their region. Because of this, the roads in the Incan road system are not uniform in width and construction methods. Another reason for the inconsistencies is that the tools and materials varied from location to location. Building techniques also had to be adapted to the conditions and terrain of the area. What is most impressive is that all of the Incan roads were built without the use of modern surveying techniques and equipment and without advanced equipment.

SECTION OF THE ANCIENT INCA ROAD IN BOLIVIA

Building the Roads

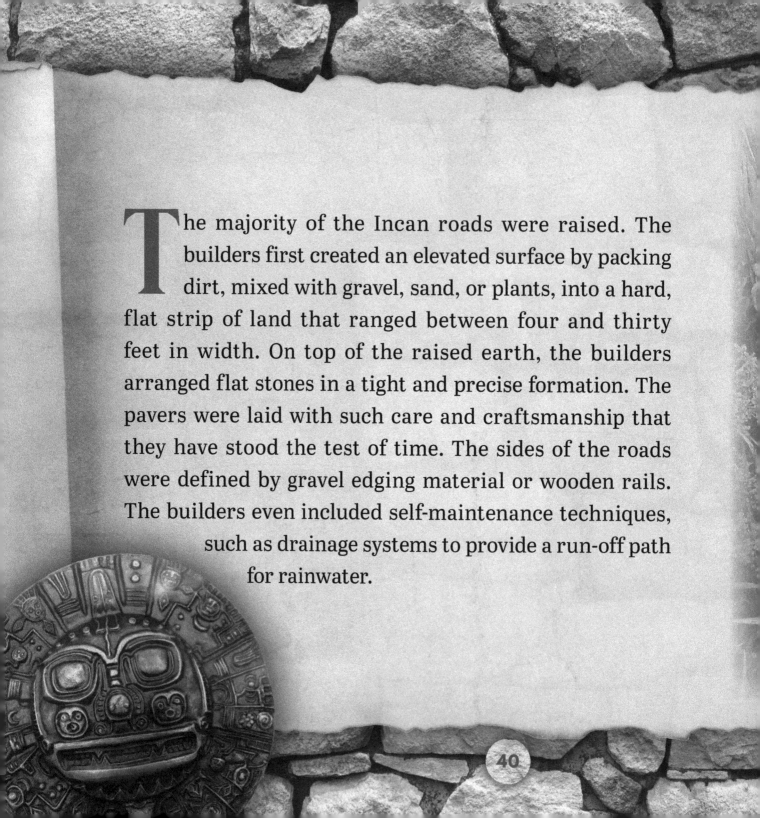

The majority of the Incan roads were raised. The builders first created an elevated surface by packing dirt, mixed with gravel, sand, or plants, into a hard, flat strip of land that ranged between four and thirty feet in width. On top of the raised earth, the builders arranged flat stones in a tight and precise formation. The pavers were laid with such care and craftsmanship that they have stood the test of time. The sides of the roads were defined by gravel edging material or wooden rails. The builders even included self-maintenance techniques, such as drainage systems to provide a run-off path for rainwater.

THE PAVERS WERE LAID WITH SUCH CARE AND CRAFTSMANSHIP
THAT THEY HAVE STOOD THE TEST OF TIME.

Winding Roads

The Incan engineers designed their road system to work with the terrain instead of against it. Many of them followed natural curves and passes in the mountains of South America.

SERPENTINE NARROW ROAD TO MACHU PICCHU, PERU.

Some of the roads were cut through the steep slopes of the Andes in a back and forth, or switchback, fashion to make the incline less drastic and easier for the travelers and their llamas to use. In many parts, the steps were cut into the rocks, but these were always made wide enough to accommodate the llamas.

THE STEPS WERE ALWAYS MADE WIDE ENOUGH TO ACCOMMODATE THE LLAMAS.

Impressive Bridges

Some of the roads that the Incan road builders constructed crosses rivers, canyons, and gorges. The Incas overcame these obstacles by building bridges. Several of the bridges were made out of stone and included buttresses[5] to support the structures. Still others were suspension bridges that were made using ropes and vines. They were strong enough for three or four travelers to cross at once.

---

[5] Buttress – A prop or support.

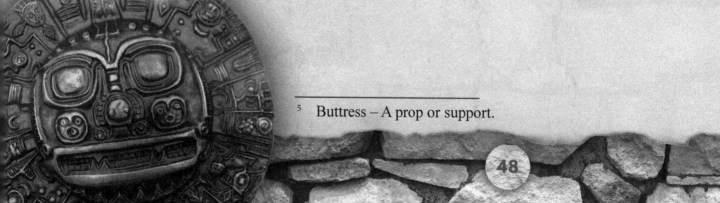

INCA ROPE BRIDGE, QUEHUE, PERU

One of the best-known Incan bridges was located near Cuzco at the Apurimac River. This bridge was nearly 150-feet in length.

QUESHUACHACA IS THE LAST REMAINING INCA ROPE BRIDGE SPANNING THE APURIMAC RIVER IN PERU.

At some rivers, two bridges were built. One was meant to be used by common travelers, while the other was reserved for the noble elite.

THE COLONIAL BRIDGE OF CHECACUPE AND THE INCA BRIDGE BUILT WITH STRAW – QUESHUA CHACA, CHECACUPE, CUZCO, PERU

Maintaining the Roads

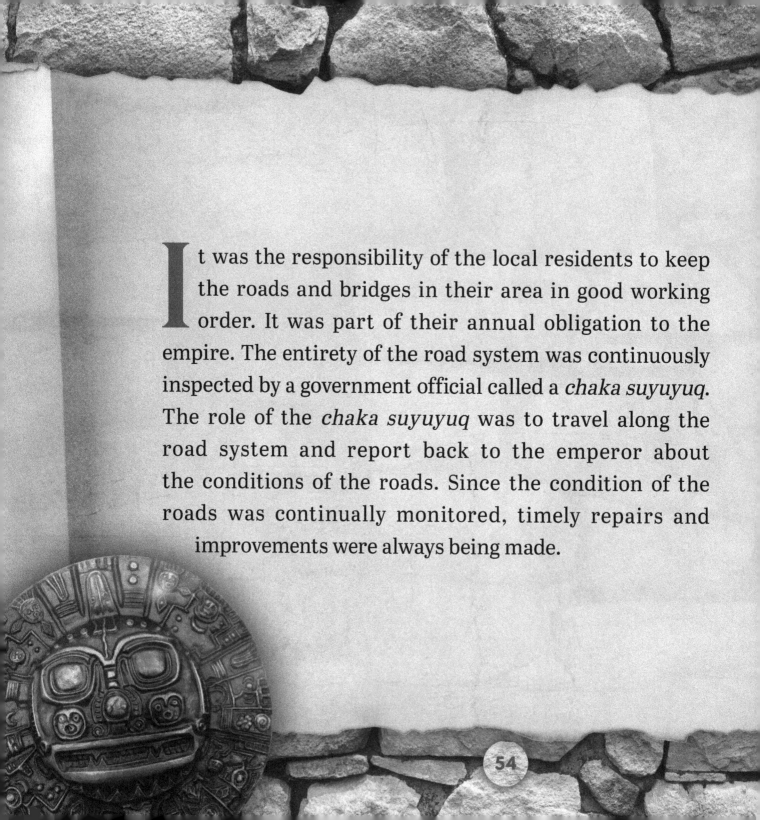

It was the responsibility of the local residents to keep the roads and bridges in their area in good working order. It was part of their annual obligation to the empire. The entirety of the road system was continuously inspected by a government official called a *chaka suyuyuq*. The role of the *chaka suyuyuq* was to travel along the road system and report back to the emperor about the conditions of the roads. Since the condition of the roads was continually monitored, timely repairs and improvements were always being made.

GOVERNADOR·DELOSPVENTESDESTER.
CHACASVIOIOCACOSINGA
GVAMBOCHACA

A BRIDGE GUARDIAN OR CHAKA SUYUYUQ IN THE INCA EMPIRE.

Using the
Roads

The purpose of the Incan road system was not to make travel easier for the common people. It was for government use. The roads made it more convenient for government officials to journey to all parts of the empire to collect taxes, take censuses, hear legal disputes, and deliver governmental communications. Common citizens were not allowed to use the roads unless it was for official government use or if they received special permission. Even then, they were required to pay a toll.

THE INCA ROADS MADE IT MORE CONVENIENT FOR GOVERNMENT
OFFICIALS TO JOURNEY TO ALL PARTS OF THE EMPIRE.

Road Runners

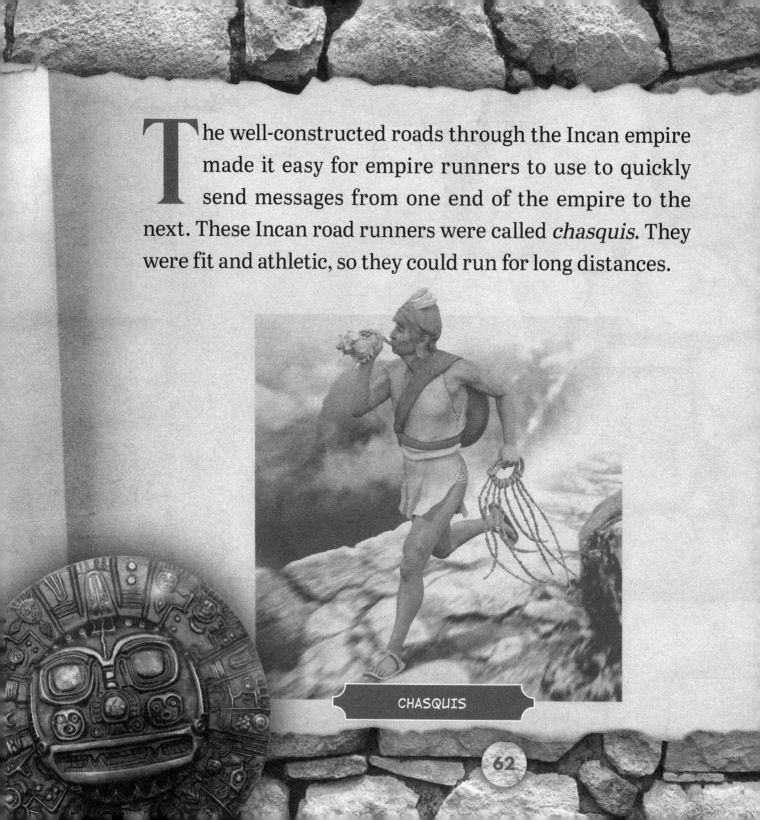

The well-constructed roads through the Incan empire made it easy for empire runners to use to quickly send messages from one end of the empire to the next. These Incan road runners were called *chasquis*. They were fit and athletic, so they could run for long distances.

CHASQUIS

DEPOCITO DEL INGA
COLLCA

They passed their message to a fresh runner posted along the route at six to nine-mile distances, so the message could move quickly through the empire. Often, the messages were delivered orally from one runner to the next. Private messages were sent using a system of knots tied onto strings, called *quipu*.

AN INCAN NOBLEMAN RECEIVES A REPORT FROM AN OFFICIAL, WHO HOLDS A QUIPU USED FOR COUNTING AND RECORDING FACTS AND EVENTS.

The Incan Roads Today

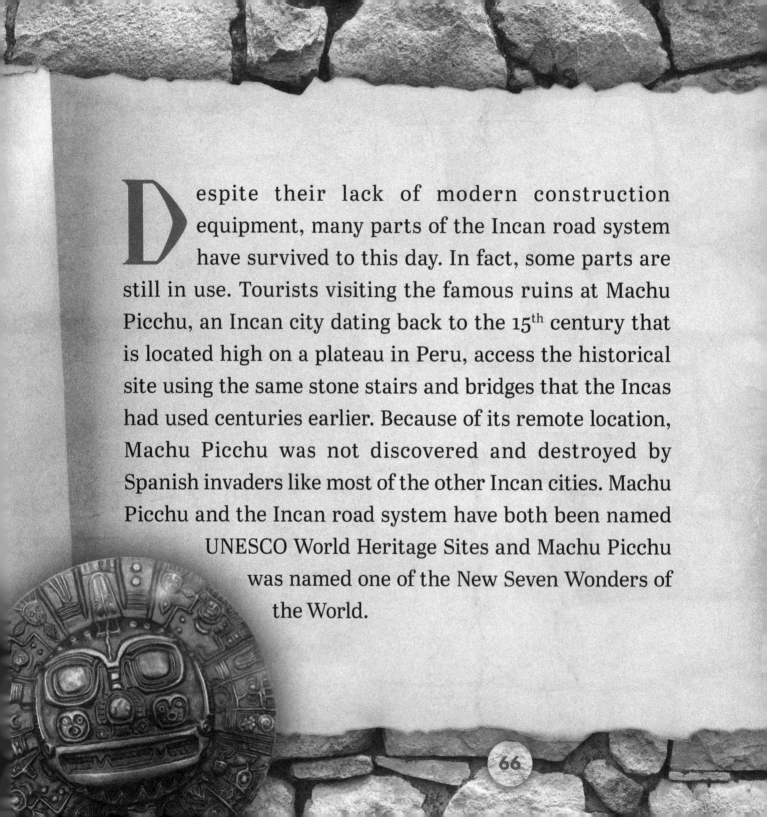

Despite their lack of modern construction equipment, many parts of the Incan road system have survived to this day. In fact, some parts are still in use. Tourists visiting the famous ruins at Machu Picchu, an Incan city dating back to the 15th century that is located high on a plateau in Peru, access the historical site using the same stone stairs and bridges that the Incas had used centuries earlier. Because of its remote location, Machu Picchu was not discovered and destroyed by Spanish invaders like most of the other Incan cities. Machu Picchu and the Incan road system have both been named UNESCO World Heritage Sites and Machu Picchu was named one of the New Seven Wonders of the World.

A FEMALE HIKER IS WALKING ON THE FAMOUS INCA
TRAIL OF PERU ON THE WAY TO MACHU PICCHU.

Summary

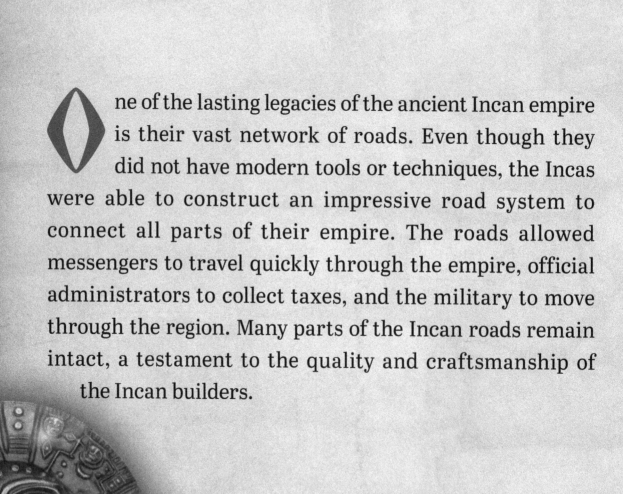

One of the lasting legacies of the ancient Incan empire is their vast network of roads. Even though they did not have modern tools or techniques, the Incas were able to construct an impressive road system to connect all parts of their empire. The roads allowed messengers to travel quickly through the empire, official administrators to collect taxes, and the military to move through the region. Many parts of the Incan roads remain intact, a testament to the quality and craftsmanship of the Incan builders.

Visit

www.speedypublishing.com

To view and download free content on your
favorite subject and browse our catalog of new
and exciting books for readers of all ages.

CPSIA information can be obtained
at www.ICGtesting.com
Printed in the USA
BVHW062057280121
599006BV00005B/330

9 781541 979857